T0380569

Circling The Abyss

Poems of Love, Nature, and Spiritual Inspiration

Curtis Church

authorHOUSE®

AuthorHouse™
1663 Liberty Drive
Bloomington, IN 47403
www.authorhouse.com
Phone: 833-262-8899

Published by AuthorHouse 11/20/2024

ISBN: 979-8-8230-3434-0 (sc)
ISBN: 979-8-8230-3433-3 (e)

Library of Congress Control Number: 2024920056

Print information available on the last page.

All interior images and cover are AI generated.

This book is printed on acid-free paper.

Contents

∘ ———— ∘ⓖ∘ ———— ∘

Dedication

This book of poems is dedicated to my mother, Elsie Patterson. She was there for my first breath as I was for her last.

Prologue

The nature of man:
Though wise as a sage
He'll die of old age
Rattling his breath
Like the bars of a cage...

Reveal

Look inside this musty tome
Read about the four-fold Om
All directions are but none
Your focus of will can be only one
The inner chamber, your mind is still
Ignore the illusion, it is not real
The layers peel back to reveal...

Ascend the mountain
And touch the tree that grows there
How sweet is its sap

Wind howls wispy off
Top mountain peaks edgy sharp
Trees slumber below

Sweet Sound The Silence

Sweet sound the silence
Water running over stones
Arriving at your footstep
I am home, I am home

Sweet sound the air
Listen to the wind
Breathe in all the life
Living once again

Sweet sound the hills
Earth echos resound
I come upon the mountain
This is holy ground

The hearth fire is warm
Her arms a close embrace
I raise my eyes to look upon
The holy mother's face

Arrow of Devotion

As the focused mind releases the arrow
To the target of devotion
The bow no longer has meaning
The hand that touches the string
Gives up its hold
The target loses its significance
And the arrow, in its flight
Becomes like a flower
Each scented petal falling away
As it encounters nothing

Sacred

Beauty awaits
In sacred heart
It opens
Like a lotus flower
And its scent
Is like heaven

Flowers love the rain
As surely as the tree grows
Water is our life

Starlight streaming through
Opals like an open door
Moonlit path to walk

Confusion

I heard the thrushes in February
Singing songs of spring
Chilly, wet dripping rain
Instead of snow
Confusion is their refrain

Blue sky clearing now
Alpine trees with tender frost
Cloudy skies return

My mind is blowing
Scattering leaves in the wind
Rain falls down on me

Despair

It's craziness, it's utter madness
This living life of drowning sadness
Faint remembrance of the gladness
Now driving you to tears

Lightning flashing, thunder crashing
Suddenly your teeth are gnashing
The crazy bedlam drowns out light
It draws you in without a fight
Hope of living fades from sight
All for naught and lost

A drum beat beating in your head
A drip drip dripping fear of dread
Slowly slowing down instead
Stillness now and nearly dead
It's quiet
Shhhh

Nothing Wrong

Sadness arises from the mind
An irrational fear of the unknown
An inward crying like a child
Refusing to eat their peas
There's a splinter in the mind
Telling you there's something wrong
There's something wrong
There's something
But what is it
But what is
What
Crying like a child at the irrational fear of the unknown
It's just fear
The fear of fear
There's nothing to be afraid of
There's nothing wrong
There's nothing

My God

My god is the feeling you get
In the spring when the sun is rising
And the green grass grows
In absolute vibrancy
And everything is radiating
Joy and love

My god is the powerful thrumming
Of the heat of the summer
When the sun bakes the earth
Like a hammer in the forge
And your skin glows warm
In the glory of its rays
As cicadas sing of long years past

My god is the changing color
Of the leaves in autumn
When the wind blows
Frosty curlicues in the morning ice
And melancholy wistfulness
Reminds us that change
Is his only constant

My god is the beautiful stillness
Of deep winter's cold
When even the river
Gives over to quiet contemplation
Of every single snowflake
That falls on its banks
Where buried seeds lay
Waiting for spring

Fate

Don't wait for serendipity to find you
Lest fate sit down and quickly bind you
With ropes and ties that karma
Makes for free

The shackles bind you
You're not free until you're not
Vision slowly clears

They sign the papers
The black ink dries like her tears
Distant birds in flight

Earth-bound Woman

Earth-bound woman, elemental
Her nature extravagant
With a knowing smile
Teach me all your ways
Your art of pleasure and
Your slender-fingered caress
Your love is sublime and passionate
An emulation of the eternal play
And I sit humbled at your feet

Promise

Janus doth stretch out his hand
And begins anew what has always been
It is covered with ice
And snow
But though the winds do blow
It will suffice
For the new days dawn
And warm spring will turn her face

Gentle skies and sun
Warm bliss falls upon our skin
While she holds my hand

In the field flowers
Grow with opportunity
They forget-me-not

Wondrous Sound

In the center of myself
There is a sound
Mystical, wondrous
Holy ground
It starts off small
A shimmering brook
And grows in brilliance
Just take a look
Now close your eyes
And sit in silence
Ripples in spacetime converge
The chakra snake
For eternity's sake
Wholeness of body preserved

Ancient Tree

Ancient tree its power flowing
Endures with arms uplifted glowing
It stands on cold dark dreary night
A fortress strong of wooden might
Twisting and streaming
And turning and dreaming
Upon sunny spires
To which all aspire
It spreads its bough toward Nuit's fold
As if seeking the truth of nature's design
Now crying tearful sap

Its roots pierce deep the grounded earth
To a seek a stable unyielding berth
And keeping pace with Gaia's best
It grasps at mortal heart's unrest
Says he, drive deep and persevere
And river's end reach you, eyes clear
But bare is the tree, in winter's grip
Silvery frost on every tip
Perseverance for naught
Where silence is taught
In the deep, dark, depths of death

However.....

Prometheus-like he has cast his leaves
Months before into an autumn breeze
And prey to gravity's vortex wide
They fell to the old tree's gnarled side
And then in melding with the earth
The leaves made rich brown living turf
A deeply layered mossy bed
Tree-sustaining, earth-rain fed
And so in emulation
Of nature's vast sensation
The tree encircled the universe

Right Now

All of it
Is in every bit of it
So rejoice in the moment
As it passes to the next
The same thing again

New day dawns again
The turning of my love finds
Awakening strength

Sunlight gleams like ice
On distant mountains rising
Heralding winter

Dichotomies

All things bound up
And all things freely swirling
Dichotomies to set the mind awhirling
And still the world is quickly twirling
All in the blink of eye

Haltingly falter
The slow response of the will
Everything is lost

Tedious waiting
The heart beats with every breath
My mind like the tide

Four Things

These four things encompass the whole
Down to the depths of the soul:

Life, death, budding rebirth
These are the things of the earth

Mind, intellect, ego's fanfair
These are the things of the air

Mother, sister, virtuous daughter
These are the things of the water

God, spirit, blindly aspire
These are the things of the fire

Wheel or gyre
It's phoenix fire
Beginning to end without goal

Alchemy

Water is the love of life
Life is the water of love
Love is the water of life
Trickling down from above
Now cultivate within yourself
The secret seed of love
Then your soul will fly away
Like a perfect, pure white dove

Love is letting go
Even though the heart doesn't
Free the soul to yearn

Snow drops settling
Mountain's vast cavernous scene
From it rivers flow

Enlightenment

In seeking will the mind begin to know
In looking will the eye begin to perceive
In contemplation will the heart begin to understand
In listening will the ear find humbleness
In quiet will you hear the word like a gentle stream
And in silence will it be spoken like thunder

Empty

When you give up trying
You will do
When you give up wanting
You will have
When you give up knowing
You will understand
And then all things
Will be in hand

Soul's aim to seek it
Mind's desire to will it
Heart's contemplation

Two stars shine their light
The radiance of which shows
A road paved with love

The Secret

The secret is revealed
In quiet solitude
It is not given
But becomes self-evident
As the layers of knowledge peal back
Until nothing remains

Blue sky opens up
Beckons the heart to follow
A fleeting moment

What sweet surrender
Is pulled from me with a kiss
From your loving lips

Ancient Realms

The lakeside lady
Dreams of forgotten realms
Where dragons old lay in wait
And venting steam rises
From ancient cracks in the facade

Lilting hand caresses her lace
Dreaming
While the silver serpent licks
Lips cracked from the dust of the earth
Old moon rises

She awakens!
New moon dawns like realization
She casts off rusty chains like
Old memories
A flaming sword illuminates her path

Heart Of Love

Lugubrious though he moves
The light from a heart of love
Illumines his days
And shows a path
Through the dark and tangled
Labyrinth of his mind
And perchance he begins to consider
That maybe
Maybe
Hope does spring eternal

Hope

There is a real rise
When you realize
That hope is eternal
That good outweighs bad
Even by just a little
And that is enough

Blossoms underneath
The deep snow of winter's chill
Lay dormant in bliss

Cold bite in the air
Seeming descent into night
Fall brings new colors

Reflection

The eye cannot see itself
Except upon reflection
But the ultimate mirror
Reflects only truth
Its cracks heal up
Until there is only one
There is no reflection
There is only you

Sitting on the edge
It has not yet been revealed
The glory beneath

The distant mountains
Reflect the dreams of my mind
The sun rises high

Life of the Light

The life of the light of the sun of the son
Gives forth in abundance its bounty
And when in advance the green grass grows
Spring does show in his face

Like the butterfly
Temperance against the dark
Colors soon return

Mist and morning dew
Freeze in frigid autumn air
Kiss of winter's bite

Fruition

The fruition of my thought
Blossoms under your care
And always its petals turn
Toward your sun

Oh my heart it hangs
By the strings you touch and hold
Cut not one my dear

Rain pours down on me
Thoughts of you become rivers
That flow to your sea

How Gently Easy

See how easily the birds fly
See how easily the wind blows
The trees and their leaves sway
So gently
From words spoken long ago

The bedrock of the earth
Cries to us
It beckons us to it's lair
Ancient foundations laid down
Deep deep springs laid bare

The arc of the cerulean sky
Holds us
Reaching outward through space
Covering us like a mother's blanket
Blessing us with its grace

And there you are
With your beating heart
Breathing, looking, listening
To the singing of birds
And the word of god
All around you, glistening
Saying
I love you

In the Beginning

In the beginning
With the telling of the story
There was a man
A man who surpassed all else
And there was not a thing that existed
Outside of himself
That was not also in him
His eyes blazed the glory of the morning
His mouth spoke the beauty of the sunrise
His beard dripped moist dew like
The finest of scented oils
His long limbs encompassed the beauty
Of all there ever was
His gentle poise bespoke the quality of silence
And behind him rose a thunderous noise
Like the sound of everything
Flowing into itself
The river of love
Emblazoned on his brow

Balance

You have to taste
The bitter and sweet
Together as one whole
Cause and effect
It goes round and round
Wrapped tight like your mother's stole

Many shades of grey
Combine in infinitude
The rainbow revealed

The early snow here
Weighs heavily on the heart
Winter is coming

Love

Love is the essence
Shared between all things
Between all sorts of people
In all sorts of ways
It's shared between the stars
And the sky
And between molecules
And atoms
But any way you slice it
It's the same thing
Love

Love is the underground movement
That keeps this world turning
The underground stream
That keeps it nourished
It is like water
It cannot be grabbed and grasped
Or it will slip through your fingers
It must be held carefully
Gently
In a cupped palm
And only then by the grace
Of gravity's subtle attraction

Love is that constant universal force
Of two becoming one
That desire to dissolve oneself
In the alchemical bowl of unity
And to forget the self
In the bliss of love
And for the sake of love

Silent Interplay

The infinite sea and infinite shore
From their silence create
Mountains of interplay
Tidal waves of possibility
Rocky pools of glorious life
Reef upon reef of civilizations
A cacophony of sound!
....That drops into a million years
....Into an ocean of silence
....Washed upon an infinite shore

Desolation

Have you ever seen the desolation
When the Earth was only rock and ice
Granite cracking and shaping under
The dense and enormous weight
Of descending glaciers
The silent creaking of ice
Echoing in your bones
Wind whispering along carved caverns
Up to crested columns of frozen spires
Down through icy valleys of jagged rock
And the cold, cold, hard stones of the earth whispering
Desolation

Forgotten Memory

Some of us are coming
And some of us are going
The old soul doesn't know where
And the new soul can't tell him
The angels keep their secrets

Silence buds in bloom
Sunrise on the hill glistens
Distant memory

My thoughts are flowing
Sunrise on the ebbing tide
Long-forgotten dream

Mind Bridges

Disperse into the vast
Consciousness is not thought
I could hold onto it
Goes on forever
And ever
Amen

Starlight night alights
Stirring boundless thoughts beyond
Million light years past

Mighty universe
It's filled with mystic pleasure
Mind's undulation

Selfless Man

Blessed is the selfless man
He serves only others
The world does not know him
And will pass him by
So seamlessly he fits
Into its weave

Blessed is the man who knows no self
The world cannot have its way
For he is naught without and within
And is part and parcel of the whole
With nothing to push on
And no center to turn about
He cannot be moved
And knows no boundaries

Blessed is the man content with himself
For him there is no end
Nor a beginning
He will slip through the cracks
As the ego fractures
Revealing the blinding light of unity
Where he is one

Tree

There is a tree
And on it grows
The most wonderful melody
A person knows
A tinkling bell
Soft wave's sigh
Chattering birds
Light of the eye
Now listen close
Keep your ear to the door
Accept the mercy
Of that distant shore

Come Baby

Come baby, we are waiting
Your gentle crib is made
Your mama's arms are warm and tight
Her soft brown eyes are shining bright
We wait to see you with delight
Please come

Come baby, the world is waiting
To show you its glory and splendor
It's not all fun, it's bitter and sweet
But the love is there, feel its heat
To be born a human is a treat
Please come

Come baby, the eternal wave
Is calling out your name
The stars reflected in your eyes
You come to us without guise
The hands that guide you they are wise
Please come

Be Bold

Be bold, young man
Take life by the hand
And then by its horns and its nose
Force not your will
But accept its plan
And follow wherever it goes

Snowboard metal gleam
Carves out the arc of the sun
Dream the eagle's crest

Cascading down it
The snow in its chute descends
Mountain thunder reigns

Love's Renewal

As the year turns
And the sunlight comes back around
Into its glory
And the ice drops away
In favor of warm fields
Full of Alaska cotton and
Forget-me-nots
I want to see your shining face
Full of joy
And laughter
And love
With an eye still turned my way

Driveway Art

Little pieces of chalk
Across the driveway
Make me step carefully
To navigate the colors
Artwork in the sun

Like children they walk
In the innocence of bliss
Face forward the sun

Shimmering summer
Sibilant it speaks softly
Sybaritic smile

Go Forth In Beauty

Beautiful woman
Beautiful girl
Go forth and love
Let your sails unfurl
You're growing up and
The winds of change fill you
Go forth in beauty

Think big, wish big and
Hold on to your dreams
You can have it all
The bottom, middle, and the cream
It's yours to have it if you want
Go forth in beauty

But be careful of life's obstacles
Watch out for those traps:
envy, hatred, greed lest
They tie you down with straps
Give love and compassion to your friends
And even to your enemies; they need it more
Oh what's in store!
Go forth in beauty

Walk With Me

Walk with me through the golden grass
Do not turn your head
Dry your tears and look at me
Into my eyes instead

And come upon the sacred lake
Where burdens are laid rest
Hold my hand, lay down your head
Upon my beating chest

And though we fight sometimes
And don't see eye to eye
We also have a fair sympathy
A subtle bond, sweet love's sigh

The homestead lies in dearest heart
Its love it has no bounds
Please accept my love, my dear
Let it grow on fertile ground

Your Mother

Loving, caring
Hard-working, sharing
She fixes every meal for you
Ties the string on both your shoes
Loves you 'til her face turns blue
She's your mother

Beautiful, patient
Foundation ancient
She's sometimes stern but loves you still
Even if you are a pill
I think it's 'cause your voice is shrill
She's your mother

Hugging, pleasing
Arms a'squeezing
She's the one who knows you best
Catches you up in her dress
Lay your head on her to rest
She's your mother

Last Breath

Mom you passed away today
And your last breath
Was as faint as a kiss
On my sleeping cheek
It was like the gasp of a young maiden
Who finds a secret valley
Hidden behind distant hills
Like the sound of a thousand stars falling
Sighing gently into the ocean
And like a puff of wind blown
Into the white sails of a crystal ship
That bears you across the sea
Away from my dock
But I am comforted by knowing
That a cracked shell
Is just a baby bird being born

Bonus Poems!

○────────○◎○────────○

The following few poems I wrote in highschool. Although not quite as polished as the others previously in the main book I wanted to include them so my complete body of poetry (with a couple of exceptions) is in one place and, hopefully, there for your enjoyment.

A Change for the Better

Dull and white, he wobbles along
the forest floor like a piece of white
lint on green cardboard paper

He is small, slow and meticulous
He inches up the thin tree branch,
and then, munches on a dull green leaf

He seems content but yet he is bored
His life is slow and dull
Black and white
He wants a change

One day he hides his homely
countenance in silken white
He becomes a recluse

As he is by himself he starts to
discover something
He finds a beauty he never knew he had
In a burst of color and brillance
he tears away his white chains

He flys away a butterfly

~ 1987

Minutes

I am of nothing
But yet something
Bringing time
To a close

And introducing
The months to the years
And the years
To the decades

I take life but yet
Make ends meet
Without me
Time would stand still

~ 1988

The Breaking of a Spork

A spork was broken today
White and shiny its slivery shards
Spread out across the table like
The fragments of someone's imagination
Bending in an arc it shakes and trembles
As pressure by an invisible hand is placed
Meticulously
And suddenly
It snaps

~ 1988

* co-written with Bligh Conway who lent me his inspiration
  and imagination

Author Biography

Curtis grew up in Bloomington, Indiana and attended Indiana University. Following his heart, his Environmental Studies degree took him to Alaska where he resided for many years, soaking up the long summers. In 2017 he relocated back to Indiana where he currently resides. He has a wife, two children, and two acres of land. When he's not chopping wood a honey-do list is always at the ready.

Printed in the United States
by Baker & Taylor Publisher Services